PULSE

PROSE POEMS

Pulse: Prose Poems
Recent Work Press
Canberra, Australia

Copyright © the authors 2016

National Library of Australia
Cataloguing-in-Publication entry
Title: Pulse / by Prose Poetry Project ;
edited by Shane Strange and Monica Carroll.
ISBN: 9780994456519 (paperback)
Subjects: Prose poems, Australian--21st century.
    Australian poetry--21st century.
    Australian prose literature--21st century.
Other Creators/Contributors:
    Strange, Shane, editor.
    Carroll, Monica, editor.
    Prose Poetry Project.
International Poetry Studies Institute, issuing body.
Dewey Number: A821.008

All rights reserved. This book is copyright. Except for private study, research, criticism or reviews as permitted under the Copyright Act, no part of this book may be reproduced stored in a retrieval system, or transmitted in any form by any means without prior written permission. Enquiries should be addressed to the publisher.

Design: Caren Florance
www.ampersandduck.com

This book was made with the support of the

International Poetry Studies Institute,
CCCR, Faculty of Arts and Design,
University of Canberra
www.ipsi.org

Cover image: Colin Knowles, *Curtains in Light*, https://www.flickr.com/photos/colink/24876048076/in/photolist-DUdfqC-E7TKE4-7fH16b-0cj7Ld-0cxoLm-37XSmP-4QB7d4

recentworkpress.com

PULSE

PROSE POEMS

by the Prose Poetry Project
edited by Shane Strange and Monica Carroll

INTRODUCTION

Shane Strange and Monica Carroll

In selecting these prose poems (the second collection by the Prose Poetry Project following 2015's collection *SEAM*) we aimed to highlight the way that this most undecidable of forms can operate beyond the bounds of both poetry and prose to occupy a space somewhere in between — being of both forms, and of neither at the same time.

   Although this anthology aims to represent some of the work of the twenty poets who are involved in the Project, the first thing readers will notice is the deliberate choice to strip each poem of its title and author, leaving the text bare on the page. This choice was made for two reasons: firstly, we wanted to show that the collaborative vigour of the Project didn't arise from any individual or select group of voices, but from the broad mixture of contributors, whose voices intermingle, reflect and amplify each other. The whole, in other words, is greater than the sum of its parts.

   The second reason, and the one from which the title, *Pulse*, evolves, was to emphasise that these works might be read less as poetry and more as a series of fragments — excerpts, if you like, from the volumes of some undiscovered library. We wanted to concentrate on the way these pieces wove threads through each other into longer fabrics: resonating images, themes, narratives, motifs, ideas and connections. We hope you can feel a 'pulse' of meaning beating through the book.

The volume has been divided into two 'sequences', each selected wholly by one of the editors. Sequence one, selected by Shane Strange, is taken from prose poems written by members of the Project between July and November 2015; while sequence two, selected by Monica Carroll, takes in poems written between November 2015 and March 2016.

Thanks are due to book designer, Caren Florance, whose ingenuity and care in regards to the material aspects of the page are always welcome.

We also gratefully acknowledge the support of the International Poetry Studies Institute, part of the Centre for Creative and Cultural Research, Faculty of Arts and Design at the University of Canberra.

SEQUENCE ONE

I stumbled into Harlem, Radcliffe Bailey asked, 'What kept you?' I had no idea. Reputations are never what they appear to be. Nineteen eighty-one, walking up Railton Road from the station to Spenser Avenue, Poets Corner, surely every city has one. Barricades and riots, the Daily Mail trumpeted anarchy, the BBC talked about riots, 'Hey white boy,' he said. 'Who me?' I asked. 'You want some blow? It all gonna kick off, might as well chill.' 'I was going to grab a beer and that's all the cash I have left.' 'Hey me too, we can both get beer, you can owe me.' He smiled, 'I know where you live.' Well of course he did, it was right next door to him, though we'd never had a chat over the garden fence — we kept different hours. He introduced me to Yellowman and Bob Marley, I introduced him to Bob Dylan and Jo Strummer, we both went to see Buddy Guy and Little Walter. He hated the blues and pawned my nineteen sixty-one Fender Strat for twenty-four hours. Twenty-four hours, it's not a lifetime but what is? I stumbled into Harlem, Kings Cross, Brixton, Niddrie, Moulscombe, cities all around the world have their places, Napoli, Ciudad Juarez, Cape Town, and then it grows, Mogadishu, Somalia, Syria, the USA... I stumbled into Harlem, Radcliffe Bailey asked, 'What kept you?' I have no idea.

Your 'Wild Man Blues' curl like a jellyroll down Decatur, while we march parallel to the Mississippi. No saints come marching in so I hold my umbrella high. Fleur de lys chasing feather boa between the buck-jumping. We're a long way from Earthquake McGoons and those early pre-Crescent days. But you won't play Dixieland now, for anyone. It's preserved as a score in Sleeper. I came here for Tennessee Williams, William Faulkner and the staircase from *Pretty Baby* in the Columns Hotel. You came for the tribute to Bechet at Preservation Hall, its haunted façade like a watercolour or chalk drawing left in the rain. You join the head of the parade, clarinet resting on your curled lower lip, but I stay in the second line, thinking of the Lee Friedlander photograph: *Young Tuxedo Brass Band, 1966*, the old men playing a funeral.

'And remember, the more you drink, the better we sound', quipped the New Orleans bluesman before the break. We were duty bound to test his authority. (Or take it on trust. What would be the difference?) Sometimes the moment *is* the music: the summer evening when the poet's soft-clipped voice reads Barbarian Pastorals against the backdrop of its origin, shadows from the topiary darkening the lawn. Such gentle force, precluding rebuff. Next up: 'Consider, please, this dish of ratatouille. Neither will it invade Afghanistan / Or boycott the Olympic Games in a huff.' Buy that man a drink.

thelonius monk brings his finger down and hooks a skin-stretch moment out to the boundaries like a kid's eyes closed waiting for his back to be drawn on by a fingernail or a wooden spoon to be brought down on bare upraised feet for what? forgetting the 8 times table? or because you woke up with that blood in your ears you never hit me because I'd learned sneaky-wise to keep everything down in my guts but you made me watch while you did it but it could've happened to me you wanted me to know it could've happened to me and still can and old thelonius with his finger in the air he knows how to borrow or maintain the blush. And it feels like that. But good.

Taxonomy: the identification of characteristics that sort instances into groups (see Carolus Linnaeus 1737). Certain events are named massacres because they fit the definition: 'indiscriminate and brutal slaughter' (see OED 1968). 1968. But you could start anywhere. For example: Port Arthur 1996. For example: Gotland 1361. Or that undefined moment in 627 when, in Banu Quranyz, all males 'old enough to have pubic hair' went to the wall. Or 6 December 1989, at the Ecole Polytechnique. Only women were chosen that time; a brutal act, but not indiscriminate. A police officer arrives at the scene to find his daughter among the dead. In a city of 3 million people, what are the odds of that? During the Gombe War, chimpanzee killed chimpanzee: is that massacre? I don't know; I'm not a philosopher. Hutu vs Tutsi (1959 to 1994); Catholic vs Protestant (1572 to 1922); Europe vs Jews (70CE to 1945). Or are those better classified as genocide? Perhaps. If it helps us make sense. I have waited all day for news from Paris. In a city of two point two million people, surely she is safe?

She will be bird-scattered. In gentleness body-breakers will feel for where the joints are resistless. Where there's no wood for wasting or soil for concealment, death is an act of generosity, fealty to quick seasons, sudden-wilting meadows, rock, rock, pelting rainless clouds. This land needs all the death it can get. Vultures spiral into unstoppable decline. Parents of dead infants sometimes quail, instead set sail tiny boats with light burdens into the runs of milky ice-melt where fishes feed.

Waste floating on the water, lives and limbs. The washup whitewash backwash. It's all still dirty. Dirty bombs, toy guns, real trouble, fake limbs. Too far away to yell back. Sand blown glass shards, mountain pirates, everything thick with meaning and completely meaningless. A glass shard screams in your sock. Just a job and it's a life and it means nothing and then it's gone. What creeps me out is how simple it all seems. Can't ask questions with a mouth full of sand so swallow some four hourly. I can't handle the truth.

We strip the fields and lanes and avenues, gather great piles of wood, straw bales, rotten doors, chairs. It's rained for months and the Calder Valley smoulders like a bad mood. Won't catch fire. I make a paper lantern from withies, tissue, PVA and an old tea light. Watch it rise in the dusk like a new planet trying to find its place in a constellation. Pyrotechnics. The most ephemeral art form. Black powder, gun powder, 'huo yao', saltpeter. A fire cracker in a hollow bamboo stick. The ability to dazzle: colour the world yellow and orange from steel and charcoal.

Somewhere else, a passenger plane disintegrates over the Egyptian desert. Somewhere else a young boy steps on a roadside IED. Nearer home your child lights a sparkler from a gas burner. Fire-writes his name for the first time in the night sky.

the valley in the poem was supposed to be wintering but it had taken me far too long to start, and that spring green once seen could not be ignored. so — nail scissors from amazon, bulk order, landed, and then I gathered the local children — just from this village and the five or six nearest-by — and sent them up the trees. they don't climb so fast these days. oh, the past. but the trees by tuesday morning were properly stark, and the dawn when angling through them looked genuinely chilly.

Call it a restricted diet: wild blue lupine. The caterpillars must have its leaves or. (In the mind's eye, plant the fields.) The caterpillars ingest the blue. To unfold. Break the chrysalis with thinnest wings. (Plant the fields.) Tremulous life.

Walking towards the falls, I passed roadworkers, sitting for their lunchtime break, who pointed ahead. I saw nothing. They spoke a language I didn't understand. One of them picked up a small stone and threw it along the track. And as it thudded into the dust, a cloud of yellow butterflies rose against the deep green jungle backdrop, making me gasp, and I turned, smiling, suddenly the compatriot, the co-worker, the linguist: '*—mon semblable, —mon frère!*'

The difference between butterfly and spud is that butterfly is to cut almost entirely in half and spread the halves apart, in a shape suggesting the wings of a butterfly while spud is (drilling) to begin to drill an oil well; to drill by moving the drill bit and shaft up and down, or by raising and dropping a bit.

Seamus Heaney dug too many potatoes. After a while he started experiencing the Jesus Christ effect — brushing clods from each spud and squinting out its features. All dust a shroud. In time, every tuber was a man, sometimes a woman. Shrunk by death and leathered by peat. Their faces never at peace but unable to tell of the tragedies that even Irish poets turn blind to.

Onion weed, garlic pastures, fecund and lush, Hardy's Tess, not quite a woman, was sent to clear the field; the walls of the cowshed held up tiled roofs full of milk-maid stories, 'There are no angels, Claire...' but the touch of his skin, bearded chin, soft fingers on your thighs, the shallow whisper of his breath in your ear, whispering words you want to hear, there are no angels here...

The angel is near: in the corner where the frame is crooked, filling your mouth like a metaphor, like a pincer movement. A drowsy shrug. A slow and sullen kiss. Half the afternoon is gone and there is nothing left but revolutions. A keening from a high flown bird come to rest on the branch near the window. A wing or two left in the leaves. A hole framed by a souring sun.

A stillness near a corner of the picture frame; a river jetty with boys practising bombies; an old car bobbing with two girls standing on the bonnet. They dive and surface, splashes of pale light. There's a beach at midday and a nearby angel. At four years old you can almost grasp a straggling feather. Your parents' talk is the tide's burble. You think of a scorpion's beautiful tail — you reached and someone batted your hand away — and of sucking an Oleander leaf, its bitterness filling your mouth like new thought. Under another Oleander you read novels with Jane. "We're like characters," she said, and all one summer you imagined a developing plot. The stillness is what was never written; what declined to stay.

From this moment on, there's no tense other than past. 'Sit here and count how many breaths you've got left.' On a nail behind the door, there's a wire coat-hanger sagging. Pink and puckering in the sink: one blunt, severed thumb. It's time to re-evaluate that decision to bank everything on one thing, for you might wash your hands every morning but they will never be clean again. A smell rises up now from the wrong side of ripeness.

Some of his best words were late words. He was always late for meals, buses, for trains. He was late for clandestine love affairs with women my mother never knew and those significant moments: family births, deaths and marriages. But these late words were a wonder. Fireworks! Well worth waiting for. He told me that the brain stores a sense of time in the cerebellum. He spoke of motor areas and basal ganglia, synapses. He told me of his love of biology and neuroscience. He told me to wallow in the present like a hot bath, in the moment. Don't try to live like Eliot. (Cautious banking is a watercolour, a pale version of a life.) Just think of that patient etherised on a table as the sun set over the Thames.

if you can't trust the future, who can you trust? if you can't trust the future, who can you trust? if you can't trust the future, who can you trust? if you can't trust the future, who can you trust? if you can't trust the future, who can you trust? if you can't trust the future, who can you trust?

John Wayne would never stand for this baloney. He'd eagle-eye from behind his eye-patch and act out another trash movie. Where is the man I never was? The one who could rescue me, then fix the latch on the back-gate to keep the goats from the corn?

What does a farmer wear? What is that thick felted zip-collared broad shouldered hay black needle-shin handshake in Christmas Eve aisle — Jack! plum pudding, Happy Christmas to you.

The farmers announce themselves with a song, then get embarrassed at their wellington boots, as we wave them in. Mulled wine. Mince pies. People have names, but which, who? They wonder what song will make their escape, and how much money for the village hall roof. The dog, at first scavenging, beats a retreat. Muddy puddles on the flagstoned hallway linger through the night.

He's up for the chop come morning. Don't ask no questions, mind. Says he wants these oranges on the table but they've not been cultivated yet. Them details of history undoing the theatre. Got the sore knee again. Scullion in rags, all I am. He nabs the glory of death. I never lived.

                                              the pig
the lips the skin the eventual gravestone
with you rubbing on it I shouldn't say but
keep colouring what goes into the sky
a flamingo I haven't seen but watched
pelicans trawl and flesh, fetch and eat I don't
know if I could put that black shirt on him

The shooter at the back door, blooded. Pig dogs howling in the back of the ute. Mate, he said, mate, help us out? And gave us Maud, an orphaned piglet in a bag. She grew up as the kids grew up, footie games in the backyard, wrestling each other for treats. When the neighbour shot her, he gave her back to us in butcher bags. We broke down her run, and burned her favourite rug, and buried what was left.

I like pigs too much to bring home the bacon. I only eat turkey bacon. My breakfast eggs riding on long, pink rashers. Rushed, rashed, eaten in haste. It's no surprise that *The Three Little Pigs* has always been my favourite fairytale and Arnold on *Green Acres* is my dream child. I envy Marie Darrieussecq's *Pig Tales* and Petunia Pig on *Merrie Melodies* — Porky Pig's girlfriend. I've told a lot of porkies but I'm not lying when I tell you I've loved Wilbur and Babe equally. I have a piggy bank, I give piggy backs, I go 'wee, wee, wee all the way home', but I find when I get there that my house is a pigsty.

Below the cast skin of the bull things were a mess. Students painted mappa mundi on its flanks. You taught me how to handle a nineteen footer, how to tack between the rocks that gave the city its name. Bull sharks in the water after cyclone season. There be dragons. Falling mangoes that smashed windscreens, date palms brushing our hair. After the second murder things grew taut between us. After the day you had the cats put down. After you fucked me on the edge of the balcony, three storeys above the gravel yard, me passive, you attentive. I wasn't really passive. I was waiting to make my move.

She said she wanted to live as in a story. Figs on a white plate; a blue ankle-length dress that creased under the arms. A few cattle moved towards the waterhole. The yellow sky was ablaze. She cut her arm with a razor blade; I made a bandage with a clean handkerchief. Cattle nudged us like familiars, smelling of earth and pasture. She turned away in disgust.

Why is a raven like a writing desk? Because both blacken mood (whatever the mood). Because a moulted or pulled quill, whetted and loaded to the gill with ink, makes the glowing deskplace a workspace and the bird denuded. Because goose, swan, turkey, eagle, owl and hawk can be elevated, though not necessarily, by uplift, by voice lifting from a white page, as a lark might.

We found old starlight lying at an angle on the cellar's clay floor. Stroking its fur we brought lustrous shreds back to its coat and stood in small glories that were a hundred flickering eyes. Eventually we watched it move outwards like a flock of birds, heading for outermost latitudes. We knew once more night's dumbstruck eloquence, and regained a fisherman's sense of the febrile sea — offering lines to the surge. Sky's cuneiform constellated in our pupils like an inoculation.

fleshier with age, the word like a weapon. flashes and points, deflects and rebounds, back into the quiver. our safety, our defence. time thrusts by air. we record its passing with arms, with legs, with torso. a recall soon as echo, soon as past. a bite when we don't take the fruit. a taste, a flip of the tongue. a warning ssshhhuhh leaves us with an undertaking understanding of the body left here.

We have sex in the pink hotel. Sometimes we are Mr and Mrs de Winter. Other times, Lord and Lady Lucan. He lets me eat the Toblerone from the mini-bar. I love the hard, honeyed pieces of nougat speckled through the chocolate. Sometimes his mobile phone rings. Occasionally, he answers it with his left hand over my mouth. Pink ring of lipstick on his palm. Other times he ignores the ringing and grinds against me. Closing his eyes for a second, his temple throbs. Once. Everything is still, except for his breathing. I start to speak, but the Toblerone has stuck my tongue to the roof of my mouth.

On the city's edge on the other side   of a
wall of trees in the tall grasses   we grasped
grappled gasped kissed and licked   a pale
winter sun   arms and legs and lips and
eyes   sighed and struck and fumbled   a
cathedral city   O joyous   impatience

Such beautiful flowers and such bitter sap on our hands. The city was ringing to the sound of gunfire and birdsong and gun fire and birdsong and what we mistook for firecrackers. My skin was reddening, itching. We learnt later of a cafe. A stadium. A gig somewhere in another arrondissment. You stretched your fingertips out and I smelt the warmth of you, the fear and warmth of you. Small spaces. A broken-backed passageway led out of our courtyard into the streets. Sirens. Policemen on corners. I could hear all the small spaces of the city and broken-backed sirens. Stay. *Please don't go back to her tonight. Such beautiful flowers and such bitter sap on our hands.*

We took the ferry from the harbour out toward Robben Island, to see the brown seals that colonise the bay. The water was grey, and the seas high. Where two oceans meet. Where oceans collide. This is not a metaphor; it is innocent geography. The other kids turned green and leaned across the rails, ribboning vomit into the sea. The crew washed the deck with seawater, drenching our shoes. I was at home on the sea. I took out my box brownie and snapped shot after shot of the silent rock ahead of us, sea birds whistling at its walls. The camera shook; the photographs failed.

I wonder if there were wunderkammers on Robben Island; little boxes holding stories from across the water, treasures of soap stone figures and beads for braiding, a lock of a lover's hair, tiny scraps of paper with names and kisses, the letters themselves long disintegrated into feathery dust or else confiscated, slivers of charcoal and chalk, maybe a pencil stub, a bottle top from the last beer before they shipped those boys out; shipping us out, shipping us in, on-water-matters matter more and more; in my wunderkammer I have a compass, just in case.

Once when we travelled you wore a key about your neck. People would stop and ask you what it opened — your heart, your home, the centre of the earth — but you insisted it was just a key that opened nothing extraordinary. Only to the Japanese waiter in the crypt at St Martin in the Fields did you allow any concession. When he asked if he might use it, you answered *perhaps*.

I remember we smoked on the concourse behind the Pittsburgh bus station. I lit your Virginia Slim with my own and didn't speak of class. We tied our wrists together and watched the ashes fall. You said, in the perverse fashion of the young, 'Age is no excuse in matters of dying'. But I was thinking of Vegas carparks, and the cool cables of the Golden Gate bridge. Though it was a ragged opportunity, a half chance at best, you clung to England like a machine for better living. But your moment lay beautiful before you like an uneaten rose. Now all I have is that tar black taste in my mouth, and a tongue that tells me the big skies are falling in to disrepair.

Bring America home and smoke it. History's prizes flatout boggle: ceilings of diamonds, sapphire floors, high walls of coral, pearl bowers, the kind of quiet a child might scoop up in a scallop shell. Graceland. Xanadu. SuperBowl. Swagger about and fill your barns with grain.

But the price is, in the long run, scaled to the whole damned planet: blood the only balm on a million million bodies; and my own life ended, with a wife plus our progeny and nothing else behind. My dust is what she's left with, only that, her body's bearing. Gunk.

You who will come along, surviving afterward, learn the nub of these four facts: (1) Time makes Hope a fool; (2) The grave obscures invigorating sun; (3) The Earth will blush before it suffers quake; (4) The last heat in cinders spends itself on an extinguished fire.

So. Down comes a stroke where the veins all start and spread. My battered body, violently slain, no longer me, is just steaming like a pot.

It's come to this. The hardest steel gets eaten soft with rust. And moss mucks all unburied bones like ivy clogging walls.

Not at all like this. Portobello beach in the sunshine, a mile long stretch of sand and sea, the fairground at one end, the beginning of Leith at the other; we walked the length, tested the water, it was freezing, always freezing, but the Drifters sounded good. It was never a bored walk. We wandered, wondered about America, you said, 'One day we'll go and it will be amazing.' Not at all like this.

Way beyond what's known, in the water that tilts off the edge of the world, are the big-lipped whale, the gold-armoured serpent, the siren of fatal sidelong looking. Pack me a bag of cheap trinkets, knit me a scarf against the screaming gale, the green foam. Send me, directionless, alone.

The monsters seem nearer these days. Smaller, but more intent. You step into familiar, sun-skimmed waters, and take the plunge. Your wristwatch flashes past your face as you twist and pull through the waves. You sense it tightening. Then it grips, and you see it's alive with tentacles that make you thrash and finally scratch it free — which is when your goggles cloud, slabbering tentacles now stuck to the lenses and blistering your face. You have to keep swimming as you tear the head off and pick away the tentacles one by one. The day has hardly begun.

A Miller's Thumb: the well known tiny fish with a disproportionately large mouth; seems, *er muijl ley'r's t'om; q.e.* in this case the mouth is a passage all round, here the mouth goes quite round; and thus, a mouth as wide as the head or body, which is the characteristick of this sort of minnow-fish. *Minnow*, as a prickly fish, seems, *er m'in houwe*; by this a puncture is made; if you touch it, it will prick you. *M', meê, mede*, herewith; *houwe*, puncture, wound, prick. Johnson derives it from the french *menue*, small!

In sand hills at night girls undid their halter tops. Boys stretched legs across gorse. The sand smelt of darkened heat, salty as an open bag of chips. Sand adhered to legs; adhered to bather straps. Someone dared a friend to swim to a buoy and his arms were scything glints. He returned safely but the friendship had expired. A girl asked for "anything"; all we had were cigarettes. She put cool hands on our backs and we were as still as hovering flies. Another girl said grace before opening baked beans, shrugging the can to her lips. The sea was phosphorescence bobbing like cast lures. Night fishermen arrived, our years caught fast in their nets.

Water-star moves to the rhythm of a boat on a new-moon tide. Summer slices its way over the Atlantic to the shore. What sun there is slowly works its way across one side of my face as I stand fishing. I like the movement and the stasis of it, the alternating cast and return breathing a line across the channel, the tide too lazy to come back from the slack. I measure afternoon and evening by the dull punctuations of the fish that roll or splash just a little too far out. All the gulls have deserted me for other silences that require breaking; the seal turns its back and swims away. Venus and Jupiter twin themselves somewhere out on the horizon. I am content that every star should find its own declension.

SEQUENCE TWO

She's on the verandah, examining the orange tree. Two more seasons and it's likely to produce good fruit. She swings a broom round, catching leaves and sand, ushering them down the steps. Three years ago he brought her here, giving her a secondhand car, patching its rust. Dinner's at six every night. A spider spins an arched web; she notices the paint's relentless green. The garden crowds her like a rogue herd of cows. The kettle in the kitchen heckles and steams.

The cup said, 'I no longer need to be held.' Only the dog was home to hear it. In this poem the dog whispered to the glare from windows on far away houses. In another poem someone denies that cups have language. If you heave open that heavy door (by the brass handle) you can break the hum of the room. The short story described the handle as less than brass and unattainable.

He lies in a bed of crisping bracken — bracken straight out of the book that he's discarded in the sun. He takes a magnifying glass from his pocket, focuses on the crinkled fronds. A half-hidden lizard squirms at the intrusion that grows to a torrid inquisition. He senses the power he has to rachet up the heat into a crime. His own skin is darkening. Unread pages of the novel begin their incendiary curl.

A strike ... a spark ... a sputtering wish ... a shiver of sunlit wind through leaves ... a procrastination ... a chalked line drawn across the board, towards whiskey's lingering scorch ... a scorpion on an anthill ... a whispered intimation of calamity or hurrah —perhaps both ... the colossal bridge splintering to matchsticks ... horses falling in slow motion into the river ... ribbons of blood ... the long, long haul to retribution and beyond

Dog tired from the nightshift, shoulders slumped and weary, but when he unslung his pit bag and coat, his strong arms opened to let us in.

Where the emptiness is. Tiny voices cry out for attention. Dare I say love. In the silence, no space for the dreams of hamsters, the dreams of mice. No room for the smallest tastes of everyday. Keep talking, beloved. Don't let the silence draw me in.

Beetles have set up home in our home. No plate is pure. They eat the soap in the bathroom. They leave their traces on floor and ceiling and wall. You said we should move out, you emptied every shelf onto the floor. Who'd have thought we had so much stuff? Some of it is lovely. Some of it has worth. It has been weeks now. We are still stepping around the crockery and linen and books. You dig out glasses and pour the wine. I hunt for pans to cook the mushrooms and the eggs. We quarrel about what should stay, and what go. Some nights the question becomes not what, but who.

Enough cabbage to feed ten, yet we were
two, not accounting for your inner sparrow.
    I eat for five. You scope for snails.

The day marked by the brevity of its light, the arrival of holiday bills through the mail slot: or so they say. The '70s sunburst clock tocks second by second, and a cat moans from under a radiator: this is winter, cold, isolate, fierce. Few have the strength to raise a knife.

                              where cows and
goats graze patterns of energy will one day
include measured thought what neuro-
theologists are working on comes back
to cricket in the summer love solitude
grass swishing wet ankles and under
under is why it's possible mycorrhizal
telephones whisper minerals through
the forest if this wasn't true i wouldn't
believe it or tell you what i can and marvel

The woman has borrowed arms and legs. She walks on a tightrope in front of the watching crowd. They stand back, as instructed, and do not attempt to become a bigger part of what is happening. Her mouth opens to breathe or scream. There isn't time to find out which before the rope dissolves into a flight of rainforest kingfishers, swooping low into the traffic, its liquid ooze.

Wobbling at the top of an aluminium ladder, he sliced through the laurel with his father's shears. Evergreen clippings took off around his face, and from the thick of it — a pigeon, with scissoring wings. Bright drops of blood on the pale green undersides of the leaves he saw were ladybirds, at which he breathed again, but set about his task with greater care, though he was up against time. The sky was darkening. Fat pearls of water gathered on the shrinking hedge like a swarm of little ghosts.

It's a hand-me-down: a green china hare that might be crouching in grass — as soldiers approach; as gunfire sputters. A pause when he gave her the box tied with ribbon, the fragile new china as cool as his lips. She kept the gift to nurse her bewitchment. Later she saw how the river rolled gently through verdant country, and she looked it up: Somme, an old name for tranquility.

there's a high wind in the valley of silver birches. your mother and your father shout at each other, with laryngitis. they are shouting for each other. the birches throw their shade to one side. on the bright pavilion you take forty calls. these are the animals that need rescue today.

Young Duck is getting ready for his first day at school. Mother Duck is quiet. 'Why are you quiet, Mother Duck?' asks Young Duck. 'Because,' says Mother Duck, 'I equate significant milestones in your life with the inevitable narrowing of opportunities in mine. It is unfair, I know, but I need a moment to retrieve myself from the existential angst that, if left festering, might consume me. (show illustration)

Junior Bear is helping Papa Bear. Together they are building a letterbox. Look at the letterbox. It is a red letter box. Junior Bear asks 'Papa Bear, why is the letterbox red?' 'Because, Junior Bear,' begins Papa Bear, 'in a class society my labour is alienated to the point where I can only show my resistance through meaningless symbols of solidarity that mask my tacit complicity with the system.' (show illustration)

It is a lovely day in the park. Little Iguana is flying a kite. Look at it soar! Baby Turtle is getting older. Look at her mature! Little Crocodile is playing with lipstick. Look at him experiment! Junior Panda knows she really likes girls. Look at her hiding! Papa and Papa Iguana are watching Little Iguana. Look at them overturn preconceptions! Little Baby Possum feels responsible for her parents' divorce. Look at her self-blaming! Daddy Ocelot feels weighed down by the tropes of masculinity. Look at him conform! It is a lovely day in the park. (show illustration)

The end of things might be this room of stone orange from the imperfect coloured glass no bigger than a sheet of newsprint left lying on the wall. One can see that hands cut and laid the flagstones rubbed away by centuries of leather clad feet. And I am thinking of my boy and how these one thousand, ten thousand, one hundred thousand pairs of hands and eyes have made this room a living place of generations for me and for him there is something in that — the humility of life. Please. Please. Put eyelets in the sky for his stars.

Rubbed between fingers, green earth pigment, squeezed and laid onto canvas. Gathered near Verona and the old city of Prun, a forest's shadow and verdancy. So often used by painters as the neutralising layer beneath pink skin, a knowledge of earth climbing into fleshy tones. In Duccio's *Annunciation* Mary's face shows it — optimism dropped away, a biliousness staring at the face of angelic command, her great blessing unpinked as she stands. And so often it's like this — flushed ideas failing, earth gathering its meadowed green.

Benediction. Incense velvets my nostrils. The swinging thurible and white smoke silhouetted against the red and yellow glass. Safe and golden, I believe in God in that haze of seconds. Wood smoke drifting across the back yard. It streams from burning branches and I believe only in fire as a salvific grace.

Choose one herb to last you forever, the one that won't pall or cloy, the one whose scent makes you see again the shimmer tarmac of the road home, the call to dinner through fly gauze, the soft drag of invisible night waves turning pebbles on their tongues, the salad dregs by the cold chop fat, the easily missed register of green to gold to crisp brown, the hallway thick with slow-cooked juices coming in from the cold. There isn't one.

Black rice, purple carrots, yellow beets. The kitchen shimmers with colour and you leave the room, perplexed. We have discarded the salad greens, but the beans are burnished gold, and the asparagus glows red. Nothing is as it should be. You will kiss me anyway — how could you not? Sesame oil spilt on the floor, grated ginger on our lips, chilli breath. Did we ever visit Thailand? What happened to us last year? I serve the meal, discordant colours compete for attention. It's as good a time as any to call an end.

I'm making a shrine to the fragment. In my acres of yard, piling toward the sun. Dispersed on grass, clogging stairs to the house, unfinished in my room. Dropped iron, shards of pinked glass, scrapped paintings irreparably torn. I'm building to jag soft wind, catching threads of sparrows' flight. To hold rain like remnants of ocean in pans of stainless steel (taking on so many hues). I'm jamming unjoinable parts — tiles to hem a bath; stretched wool that gathered a neck; weapons-grade glass; a split suitcase; fittings to siphon steam. I lather the present with tints of mould and foxed brown. The too much used-up; rust to darken the seen.

Blue twilight unfurls its splendour, a Didionesque gloaming for the lonely. I try to catch its tint in my cup, to taste its calm, but its inkiness spills over me until I am glass. Bathed in owl-light, I float on short blue wavelengths. I cannot be broken.

I reached into the sky
and plucked a scythe from the cheek of
the moon. Light bled into my fingertips,
travelled along my arm, across collarbone,
into my heart. I used it to cut through skin
and flesh — the blood that spilled shone
with moonlight, it whispered your name
as it spread into a dark and thirsty earth.

The city's reach pulled us, the southern sun burned without diminishing. The moon didn't rise tonight. There was poetry on the radio as blue Monday drifted into Tuesday, Wednesday. When you caught the clock with outstretched hands, I took my sharpened pencil as a lover. Good wood. You said 'I have now revised a poem to make it more specific'. I recycled, signed petitions, remembered when we were pressed together in the busy vaporetto. Your orange silk skirt.

In the room with mirrored walls, we danced with words, catching sunlit glimpses of ourselves as we sashayed and side-stepped and spun. Exuberance spent, we stepped out on the terrace to test our phrasing, the humid air held us close till words found their right places, and the sky widened with the possibility of other rooms, of abundant gardens to explore on other days. Out of the silence the bright murmur of your voice, 'I am here, I am here, I am here', a string of amber beads around my neck.

Brown pennies, red telephone box coins, days between calls; press button A and pray her father doesn't pick up; coins gone for another week, 'You didn't call.' 'I did.' Too shy to speak to her mother. Walking past your door, kicking a ball against your wall, hanging around in the dark and cold, lampost light picking out the drizzle of another Saturday night, on the other side of closed curtains that you never looked out of. One day I will fly away from this place.

Red is a towel tied on a rail near change rooms; and the thongs of a girl flap-flapping her way to shower. And sunset, raddled with too much seeing, bathing a gull. It's your anger one unforgettable afternoon; and of this evening's longing starting in the chest. A child pushes a flaming beach ball; a blushing icy pole melts in sand. It's what the fire in the beach's 44-gallon drum repeats — the colour of dropped words; the wrapped wound of a scarf.

Once there was a golden ship on a golden sea, and when the sunset ended, the ship sank.

It starts with the murmuring of blood through veins and arteries, the fluttering of vessels and butterfly wings — heat gathers just below the throat, a gentle thrumming, vibration, spreads outwards and upwards till air and skin kiss along the buds of tongue and roof of mouth — the mind a cavern, the heart a stage, the eyes are skylights — lips tingle and part to release the butterflies — they fly in circles then tuck into ears, descending till they float again through the blood stream.

To start again is the hardest thing, to leave behind the pock marks of memory. I think of the time I left you on the side of a road to thumb your way from east to west. There were three letters that year, each one grimy and creased from where you carried them too long. I think of the first time you came to meet my train, unexpectedly, and I had already left the station. I waited for you on the steps outside your apartment with the smell of cannelloni beans cooking somewhere nearby. There was one other time, at the airport, when you went to the wrong terminal, but I waited knowing you would come.

No-one's heart in that room is waiting to be broken for the first time and no-one is standing here among the quiet men whose long souls have begun to shrink in a genteel manner. Scars healing create the same effect, by slow tightening as the first wound begins to dry. In another place, to which reference was made earlier, cardiographic studies have shown how hearts not damaged are so rare it is quite possible that, statistically speaking, they may not exist at all.

I begin at night. I paint my skin and the hairs of my body and of my head. Now the sun is rising and bright hairs fall, flakes of skin fall all around me as a glittering dome. And I have the peoples' eyes, they come in and are an audience. The sun is rising, the head throbs. They are collapsing the fence. They are spilling into an air zone. Now I name the secretions of my rivals. This one bleeds. This one's nose dribbles as he cries. They are for devouring. It's rising. Flakes of skin fall. The clamour is an open breath and casts a shadow. The body shines.

Head back. Tongue out. Tasting what subtleties? The ratios of fragrant air? Descartes' corpuscular space? So happy in this gesture. Life must be felt on the tongue. Wrapped around the palatine uvula. Drizzled down the back of the throat. Or held against the roof of the mouth, forcing a melting away. Umami: the taste of the smell.

The more I feel the more I have room for no-one when the womb jerks for toothless babies with starfish hands and beady trusting eyes and the heart pangs for the mothers whose arms released of their burdens fly upwards in distress and the bowels shrink for menfolk one part invisible one part feared who having lost all want something in their fist. My heart is not strong enough for this.

I describe. I send children to the trees. I make them look into the sun. I harvest their corneas to sell on *La Caminata* to people in finely cut clothes. Pro-fesion-al. Tell me what you see. 'Everything is light' Really? For the children, tell me what you see. 'I see nothing.' They pay me in gemstones. For the children. To make eyes for the children.

The warm trilobite blaze down my left side. The hard striation, organs making way. For ever I am yours, poor jutish length of gut. Caught like a rat in your *thrum thrumming*. Taut strings folding me in two. Set at tension like a rope around a capstan. Brutal music from the Lower Cambrian. A rock stain crushed in the wind. Whatever they find will sound like history.

Reaching down, you trim your toenails with a particularly sharp poem, catching the leavings in yesterday's paper. You are sure this is not the proper use of poetry, but nothing does as good a job of preventing ingrowing.

Nothing annoys me more than the way you put all the poems in the sink after dinner. I prefer to wash them one at a time, but you pile them up and I can hear them, clinking against one another, chipping and cracking. You start scrubbing away at the sticky bits in the corners, holding each one up to the light, shaking your head and then dipping it back in the water. I could tell you that no amount of scrubbing with a steel wool scourer is going to help, but I'll let you work it out yourself. Much later, I take the poems out of the draining rack and polish them with a tea towel. They squeak when they are dry and I pile them up in the cupboard for tomorrow.

Roll up your thinnest for packing wounds that won't stop bleeding. For exsanguination of arch conservatives, apply free verse to the backs of their heads while they're banning something. To induce quiet, or boredom as it's otherwise known, in the overstimulated, or poets as they're otherwise known, ensure the poetry is entirely derivative before setting up an IV — it's the only way you can get enough of that shit into them to have any effect.

To train a poem in accountancy, suggest the merest chance that they might be sold. Poems who have never before contemplated the vulgar realm of currency, suddenly become well versed in mental arithmetic and double entry bookkeeping. It is not that the poem needs the money as such, but the validation that comes with a fair price reveals a deeper secret: that all poems just want to be loved. The secret of exchange is that it is the sincerest form of flattery.

There aren't many uses for poetry, despite all those poems that assert the contrary. If it's a way of filling the mouth of its own saying, that's not always much better than a cotton wad in a dentist's chair — and what poems do to the teeth is better left unsaid. I met a man who imbibed poetry 12 hours a day, and he could barely speak — he was so chock-a-block with dark, gnomic utterance. His dentist tried to clean his mouth but the surgery floor was badly stained by the outpourings, and his mouth was still as dark as ever, even after an hour of excavation. The dentist's prognosis was that poetry, by-and-large, is not susceptible to modern dental technology, and that it made nothing happen, etc, but the dentist himself had been reading a volume at lunch-time, and he too might have been speaking in riddles. If I deciphered his babble correctly the patient concluded that, like many other addictions, poetry was a way of learning to die. He smiled as he said it and a strange redolence spilled from his mouth.

The author would like to recall one of his recent prose poems. Sadly, he cannot identify which. Revisiting them, each seems increasingly tarnished, with the random timing of his perusals key to the dispiriting, seemingly chemical effect. Which is spreading. Only yesterday, he caught sight of a once silver photo frame on his mahogany wardrobe, turning to brass, as if the untraceable culprit of a poem was getting a grip on everything, dragging it into the dirt.

INDEX OF FIRST WORDS

CASSANDRA ATHERTON

Your 'Wild Man Blues' curl
I like pigs too much
We have sex in the pink hotel
Blue twilight unfurls its splendour
Nothing annoys me more

OWEN BULLOCK

the pig the lips the skin
fleshier with age
where cows and goats graze

ANNE CALDWELL

We strip the fields and lanes and avenues
Some of his best words were late words
Such beautiful flowers and such bitter sap
The city's reach pulled us

MONICA CARROLL

Seamus Heaney dug too many potatoes
John Wayne would never stand
He's up for the chop come morning
The cup said, 'I no longer need to be held.'
Enough cabbage to feed ten

OLIVER COMINS

The woman has borrowed arms and legs
No-one's heart in that room

JEN CRAWFORD

the valley in the poem
The difference between butterfly and spud

What does a farmer wear?
A Miller's Thumb
there's a high wind in the valley
Once there was a golden ship
I begin at night

LUCY DOUGAN

Once when we travelled

CARRIE ETTER

Call it a restricted diet
On the city's edge
The day marked by the brevity of its light

NILOOFAR FANAIYAN

I reached into the sky and plucked
It starts with the murmuring of blood

ROSS GIBSON

From this moment on there's no tense
Bring America home and smoke it

STEPHANIE GREEN

To start again is the hardest thing

PAUL HETHERINGTON

A stillness near a corner
She said she wanted to live
We found old starlight
In sand hills at night
She's on the verandah, examining the orange tree

It's a hand-me-down
Rubbed between fingers
I'm making a shrine to the fragment
Red is a towel tied on a rail
There aren't many uses for poetry

PENELOPE LAYLAND

She will be bird-scattered
Why is a raven like a writing desk
Way beyond what's known
Choose one herb to last you forever
The more I feel the more I have room

NIGEL MCLOUGHLIN

Water-star moves to the rhythm

ANDREW MELROSE

I stumbled into Harlem
Onion weed, garlic pastures
I wonder if there were wunderkammers
Not at all like this. Portobello beach
Dog tired from the nightshift
Brown pennies, red telephone box coins

PAUL MUNDEN

'And remember, the more you drink
Walking towards the falls
if you can't trust the future
The farmers announce themselves
The monsters seem nearer these days
He lies in a bed of crisping bracken
A strike ... a spark ... a sputtering wish ...

    Wobbling at the top of an aluminium ladder
    The author would like to recall

MAGGIE SHAPLEY

    In the room with mirrored walls

SHANE STRANGE

    thelonius monk brings his finger down
    The angel is near
    I remember we smoked
    Young Duck is getting ready
    The end of things might be this room
    Head back. Tongue out
    I describe. I send children to the trees
    The warm trilobite blaze
    Reaching down, you trim your toenails
    To train a poem in accountancy

JEN WEBB

    Taxonomy: the identification of characteristics
    The shooter at the back door
    Below the cast skin of the bull
    We took the ferry from the harbour
    Where the emptiness is
    Beetles have set up home in our home
    Black rice, purple carrots

JORDAN WILLIAMS

    Waste floating on the water
    Benediction. Incense velvets my nostrils
    Roll up your thinnest for packing wounds

NOTES

Jen Crawford, 'The Miller's Thumb': Kerr, John Bellenden. *A Supplement to the Two Volumes of the Second Edition of The Essay on the Archaeology of our Popular Phrases, Terms and Nursery Rhymes.* London: James Ridgeway, 1840 & 'The difference between butterfly and spud': http://the-difference-between.com.

A version of Niloofar Fanaiyan's poem 'I reached into the sky' appeared in *Otoliths*, issue 41, 2016 http://the-otolith.blogspot.com.au/

BIOGRAPHIES

THE PROSE POETRY PROJECT (PPP) was created by the International Poetry Studies Institute (IPSI) in November 2014 with the aim of enabling participants to engage in practice-led research into prose poetry and to write prose poems collegially and collaboratively. The project investigates the form and composition of prose poetry and has yielded both creative and research outcomes. It also explores reasons for the resurgence of interest in the prose poem over recent decades. To date, the Project group has members from Australia and the UK, a selection of whom are represented in this anthology.

CASSANDRA ATHERTON is an award-winning writer, academic and critic. She has written eight books (with two more in progress) and has been awarded a Harvard Visiting Scholar's position from 2015–2016. http://cassandra-atherton.com

OWEN BULLOCK's publications include *urban haiku* (Recent Work Press, 2015), ***breakfast with epiphanies*** (Oceanbooks, NZ, 2012) and *sometimes the sky isn't big enough* (Steele Roberts, NZ, 2010). He won the Canberra Critics' Circle Award for Poetry 2015. He is a PhD Candidate in Creative Writing at the University of Canberra.

ANNE CALDWELL is a poet, lecturer in Creative Writing at the University of Bolton in the UK and Deputy Director of the National Association for Writers in Education (NAWE). Her latest poetry collection is *Talking with the Dead* (Cinnamon, 2011).

MONICA CARROLL is a writer, poet and post-graduate student at the University of Canberra. Her creative work has been widely awarded and anthologised within Australia and abroad. Her research interests include phenomenology, touch, poetics and space.

JEN CRAWFORD's poetry publications include 3 (Five Islands Press, 2000), *Bad Appendix* (Titus Books, 2008), *Pop Riveter* (Pania Press, 2011) and *Koel* (Cordite Books, 2016). She is an Assistant Professor of Creative Writing at the University of Canberra.

OLIVER COMINS lives and works in West London. His early poetry is collected in *Playing Out Time in an Awkward Light* (Mandeville Press) and *Anvil New Poets Two* (ed. Carol Ann Duffy). A short collection (*Yes to Everything*) won a Templar Portfolio Award in 2014. His latest collection *Staying in Touch* is published by Templar Poetry (2015).

LUCY DOUGAN's books include *Memory Shell* (5 Islands Press), *White Clay* (Giramondo), *Meanderthals* (Web del Sol) and *The Guardians* (Giramondo), and her prizes the Mary Gilmore Award, the Alec Bolton Award and short-listings for the 2015 Queensland Premier's Prize for Poetry and the 2016 Victorian Premier's Prize for Poetry. She currently works for Westerly at UWA and also teaches creative writing at Curtin.

CARRIE ETTER is an American poet resident in England since 2001. Her poetry collections include *The Tethers* (Seren, 2009) and *Divining for Starters* (Shearsman, 2011). Her collection *Imagined Sons* (Seren, 2014) was shortlisted for the Ted Hughes

Award for New Work in Poetry from The Poetry Society. She is Senior Lecturer in Creative Writing at Bath Spa University.

NILOOFAR FANAIYAN Having lived in the US, the Netherlands, and Tanzania, Niloofar currently lives in Canberra where she has recently completed a PhD in creative writing at the University of Canberra. She writes poetry and short fiction.

ROSS GIBSON is Centenary Professor in the Faculty of Arts & Design at the University of Canberra. His books include *26 Views of the Starburst World* (2012), *The Summer Exercises* (2008) and *Seven Versions of an Australian Badland* (2002). His most recent book of poetry *Stone Grown Cold* (2015) is published by Cordite Books.

STEPHANIE GREEN is a cultural historian and creative writer, her most recent publication is *The Public Lives of Charlotte and Marie Stopes* (Pickering & Chatto, 2013). She is also the author of *Too Much Too Soon* (Pandanus Books, 2006), a collection of short stories, and a widely published essayist. She is Deputy Head of School in the School of Humanities at Griffith University.

PAUL HETHERINGTON is Head of the International Poetry Studies Institute (IPSI) and Professor of Writing in the Faculty of Arts and Design at the University of Canberra. He edited three volumes of the National Library of Australia's four-volume edition of the diaries of the artist Donald Friend and is founding co-editor of the international online journal *Axon: Creative Explorations*. He has published ten full-length poetry collections, most recently *Burnt Umber* (UWA Publishing, 2016).

PENELOPE LAYLAND is a doctoral student in poetry at the University of Canberra. She has published two books of poetry: *The Unlikely Orchard* (Molonglo Books) and *Suburban Anatomy* (Pandanus Books). She has worked as a journalist, speechwriter and as a communications professional.

NIGEL MCLOUGHLIN is Professor of Creativity and Poetics at the University of Gloucestershire. He is a prize-winning Northern Irish poet with five collections of poetry in print—including *Disonnances* (bluechrome, 2007) and *Chora: New and Selected Poems* (Templar, 2009).

ANDREW MELROSE is Professor of Children's Writing at the University of Winchester, UK. He has over 150 film, fiction, non-fiction, research, songs, poems and other writing credits, including 33 scholarly or creative books. He is currently working on *The Boat,* an extended poem, book and exhibition about people migrating to safer countries on boats http://theimmigration-boat-story.com

PAUL MUNDEN is Postdoctoral Research Fellow (Poetry & Creative Practice) at the University of Canberra. He is General Editor of *Writing in Education* and *Writing in Practice*, both published by the National Association of Writers in Education

(NAWE), of which he is Director. *Analogue/Digital*, a volume of his new and selected poems, was published in 2016.

MAGGIE SHAPLEY is a Canberra poet and University Archivist at the Australian National University. She won the 2003 ACT Writers Centre Poetry Award and her poems have been published in literary journals, anthologies and on Canberra buses as co-winners of the Poetry in Action Prize 2007 to 2009.

SHANE STRANGE is a doctoral candidate in writing at the University of Canberra where he also tutors and lectures in writing and literary studies. His research interests include creative labour and cultural work; subjectivity and creative practice and cultural representations of the city. He is a writer of essays, short fiction and creative non-fiction and now, prose poetry.

JEN WEBB is a writer and cultural theorist, and Director of the Centre for Creative and Cultural Research at the University of Canberra. She writes poetry, researches creative practice, and makes and exhibits artist books. Her most recent books are *Watching the World* (with Paul Hetherington) (Blemish Books, 2015) and *Researching Creative Writing* (Frontinus, 2015).

JORDAN WILLIAMS is Associate Professor of Writing at the University of Canberra. She pursues an ongoing interest in the future directions of reading and writing including new forms such as new media writing as well as the growing popularity of older forms such as the graphic novel, and the nexus between fiction and non-fiction.

More Recent Work

Owen Bullock — *Urban Haiku* (2015)
River's Edge (2016)

Paul Hetherington — *Gallery of Antique Art* (2016)

Niloofar Fanaiyan — *Transit* (2016)

Prose Poetry Project — *Pulse* (2016)

Jen Webb — *Sentences from the Archive* (2016)

Monica Carroll, Jen Crawford, Owen Bullock & Shane Strange — *5, 6, 7, 8* (2016)

Shane Strange — *Notes to the Reader* (2015)

all titles available from
recentworkpress.com

RECENT
WORK
PRESS

www.ingramcontent.com/pod-product-compliance
Lightning Source LLC
Chambersburg PA
CBHW022228010526
44113CB00033B/703